SandCastle™

Perfect Pets

Brilliant

Birds

Mary Elizabeth Salzmann
AUTHOR

C.A. Nobens
ILLUSTRATOR

Consulting Editor, Diane Craig, M.A./Reading Specialist

ABDO
Publishing Company

Published by ABDO Publishing Company, 4940 Viking Drive, Edina, Minnesota 55435.

Printed in the United States.

CREDITS

Edited by: Pam Price

Concept Development: Nancy Tuminelly

Cover and Interior Design and Production: Mighty Media

Photo Credits: BananaStock Ltd., Corbis Images, Luiz C. Marigo/Peter Arnold, Inc., ShutterStock

LIBRARY OF CONGRESS CATALOGING-IN-PUBLICATION DATA

Salzmann, Mary Elizabeth, 1968-
  Brilliant birds / Mary Elizabeth Salzmann ; illustrated by C.A. Nobens.
    p. cm. -- (Perfect pets)
  ISBN-13: 978-1-59928-744-7
  ISBN-10: 1-59928-744-7
  1. Cage birds--Juvenile literature. I. Nobens, C. A., ill. II. Title.

  SF461.35.S25 2007
  636.6'8--dc22
                              2006033248

SandCastle™ books are created by a professional team of educators, reading specialists, and content developers around five essential components—phonemic awareness, phonics, vocabulary, text comprehension, and fluency—to assist young readers as they develop reading skills and strategies and increase their general knowledge. All books are written, reviewed, and leveled for guided reading, early reading intervention, and Accelerated Reader® programs for use in shared, guided, and independent reading and writing activities to support a balanced approach to literacy instruction.

SandCastle Level: Transitional

LET US KNOW

SandCastle would like to hear your stories about reading this book. What is your favorite page? Was there something hard that you needed help with? Share the ups and downs of learning to read. We want to hear from you! To get posted on the ABDO Publishing Company Web site, send us e-mail at:

sandcastle@abdopublishing.com

BIRDS

Millions of people have pet birds. Most pet birds are brilliant in two ways. They are smart, and they have brightly colored feathers.

Michelle teaches her bird to talk by holding it close and saying the words she wants it to learn.

Jared gives his birds fresh food and water every day. They eat birdseed plus some fruits and vegetables.

Vanessa keeps her bird's cage clean. She changes the paper in the bottom of the cage and washes the food and water dishes.

Trevor makes sure his bird has a variety of toys to play with so it won't get bored.

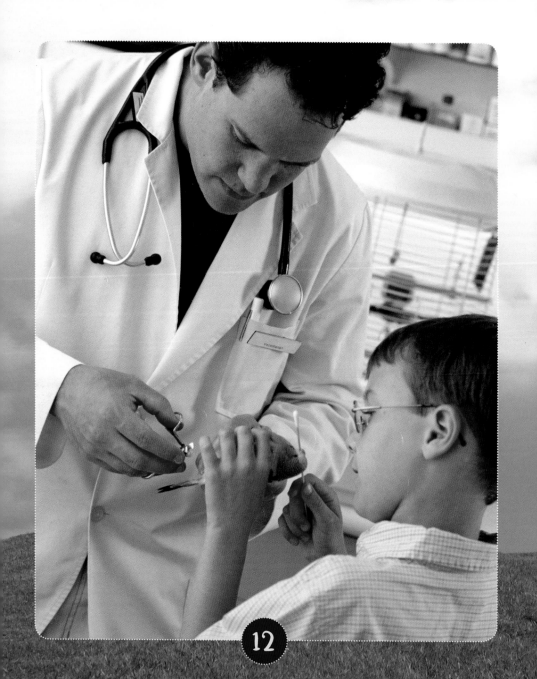

Owen takes his bird to the veterinarian for a checkup and to have its nails trimmed.

A Bird Story

Kim's bird is named
Good-Bye Ty
because he only
says good-bye.

Kim wants her bird
to learn to say
another word.

Kim would like
Ty to know
how to say
the word *hello*.

She holds him up
so he can hear,
and repeats hello
loud and clear.

But still, when Kim
gets home from school,
Ty says good-bye
from his perch on a spool.

Kim says, "Even if that
is all you say,
I will love you anyway."

Then as Kim turns
around to go,
Ty flaps his wings
and squawks, "Hello!"

Kim says, "I can't believe
what I just heard!
Ty, you are such a
brilliant bird!"

Fun facts

One of the most popular pet birds is the parakeet, which is also called a budgerigar, or budgie.

There are more than 9,000 species of birds, and 300 of them are different types of parrots.

Large parrots can live as long as people do.

People have been keeping birds as pets for thousands of years.

Some parrots are loud enough to be heard from a mile away.

Glossary

checkup – a routine examination by a doctor.

flap – to move up and down or back and forth.

perch – to sit or stand on the edge of something.

repeat – to do or say something again.

trim – to cut a little bit off of something.

variety – a collection of different types of one thing. An assortment.

veterinarian – a doctor who takes care of animals.

About SandCastle™

A professional team of educators, reading specialists, and content developers created the SandCastle™ series to support young readers as they develop reading skills and strategies and increase their general knowledge. The SandCastle™ series has four levels that correspond to early literacy development in young children. The levels are provided to help teachers and parents select appropriate books for young readers.

Emerging Readers
(no flags)

Beginning Readers
(1 flag)

Transitional Readers
(2 flags)

Fluent Readers
(3 flags)

These levels are meant only as a guide. All levels are subject to change.

To see a complete list of SandCastle™ books and other nonfiction titles from ABDO Publishing Company, visit www.abdopublishing.com or contact us at: 4940 Viking Drive, Edina, Minnesota 55435 • 1-800-800-1312 • fax: 1-952-831-1632